Soap Making Recipes Book 2: Melt and Pour Soap Recipes

By

Angela Pierce

Table of Contents

Introduction 5

Part 1. Benefits of Making Soaps at Home 6

Part 2. Recipes 8

    1. Calamine Lotion Soap Recipe.. 9

    2. Vanilla and Bay Berry Soap Bar 10

    3. Easter Egg Recipe 12

    4. Anti-bacterial Melt and Pour Soap Recipe................... 17

    5. Swirl Melt and Pour Cubes Soap Recipe 19

    6. Tea Rose Beauty Soap Recipe 24

    7. Mint Leaf Soap Recipe 26

    8. Beautiful Color Layered Soap Recipe 28

    9. Oat Meal Recipe 32

Thank You Page 34

Soap Making Recipes Book 2: Melt and Pour Soap Recipes

By Angela Pierce

© Copyright 2014 Angela Pierce

Reproduction or translation of any part of this work beyond that permitted by section 107 or 108 of the 1976 United States Copyright Act without permission of the copyright owner is unlawful. Requests for permission or further information should be addressed to the author.

This publication is designed to provide accurate and authoritative information in regard to the subject matter covered. This work is sold with the understanding that the publisher is not engaged in rendering legal, accounting, or other professional services. If legal advice or other expert assistance is required, the services of a competent professional person should be sought.

First Published, 2014

Printed in the United States of America

Introduction

Soaps not only gives you the feeling of beauty, but it also enhances your mood with heart touching fragrances. Women are always remain conscious of the products they use and what they contain to beautify them more for longer. This consciousness has turned people into a new hobby, which is soap making at home. This hobby not only provide them a creative satisfaction, but also an aesthetic sensation when they made the soaps themselves being completely aware of what does soap actually contain. There are different types of soaps making processes, which could be easily adopted to make soap at home.

Part 1. Benefits of Making Soaps at Home

You may have been thinking about the idea of soap making at home as a little weird, as when you can easily get them from stores, then why bother yourself to make them at home. Well, you concern is quite right, but let me show you why soap making at home is much better than buying them from stores:

1. You can easily customize your soap by using products which are more suitable for your skin and hence can get a better solution for your skin beautification utilizing best ingredients with complete satisfaction.

2. It will save you from long trips to the stores and will also save your money and time.

3. You can easily customize the soap with not only utilization of different ingredients but by giving them different shapes.

4. You can gift them to your family and friends, in fact they are the best gifts for Christmas and Easters.

5. You can spend your time in doing some creative activity which will quite self-satisfying and also a lot of praise gathering thing among your social circle.

6. You can make soap according to your preferences and specifications.

7. It may be superior in quality than the ones available in stores.

8. You can add fragrance of your choice and can make yourself feel better while bathing.

9. Soap making process hygiene is controlled by you and hence it will provide you more satisfaction and happiness, while utilization of homemade soap.

10. It will keep you aware of what products are better for you and hence make you a better decision maker when it comes to choose the things available at stores.

11. It could be a good hobby for your kids in summer too.

These are some of the benefits of preparing soaps at home and hoping that some of them are quite relatable to you.

Part 2. Recipes

These soaps are quite simple to make as compared to other type of soaps, because all you have to do is to get a melt and pour soap base and some fragrances of your choice to prepare eye-catching and heart-touching soaps at home. Melt and pour soaps are also considered as casting or glycerin soaps. You can easily purchase soap base from nearby store or you can place your order online to get the base of your choice.

There are many ways to make melt and pour soaps. You can customize not only ingredients of the soap, but also shape and fragrance of the soap too. For a quick start, let's show you some easy and handy recipes of making Melt and pour soaps, which can be easily customized according to your requirements whenever you want. These recipes are easy to follow and give you enough idea of how you can customize them further.

1. Calamine Lotion Soap Recipe

Ingredients:

- 2 tbsp. of Calamine Lotion

- ½ Oz Bubble gum FO

- Vitamin E (5 capsules)

- 12 Ounces of goat milk soap or Glycerin

- 2 drops of FDC Red no. 40

Preparation time: 30 minutes and settle down soap, until cool to cut into bars.

Directions to Prepare:

Melt the 12 ounces of glycerin or goat milk soap base into a boiler and add to it 2 tbsp. Of calamine lotion. The soap will get a pinkish color, to enhance it more add in it 2 drops of FDC red. Then add in it 5 vitamin E capsules plus bubblegum FO. Now, take a soap mold of any shape and pour this mixture into the mold to cool down. When it settles down and cooled well, cut it into bars. Your melt and pour soap is ready to use, so enjoy this pretty easy recipe and try it at home.

2. Vanilla and Bay Berry Soap Bar

A good soap to try out for Christmas time.

Ingredients:

- Melt and pour soap base (clear)

- Melt and pour soap base (opaque)

- Vanilla and bayberry fragrances

- Soap colorants

- Cooking spray for mold release

- Soap mold of your choice

Instructions:

1. Take a soap mold and spray in it the cooking spray, wiped away the extra oil with tissue paper. You can take mold of any shape and size.

2. We will prepare the two batches of soap with different colors. Here we are using light and dark green color shades, to give soap two different looks, you can use the color of your choice. Melt the soap base and

divide it into two parts. In one part add lime green color, while in other part add dark green color.

3. Simultaneously, ass vanilla fragrance in one part and bay berry in another part.

4. Now pour both colored soap mixture into the mold and left them until cool

5. Take out of the mold and enjoy your two color plus fragrance soap at home.

3. Easter Egg Recipe

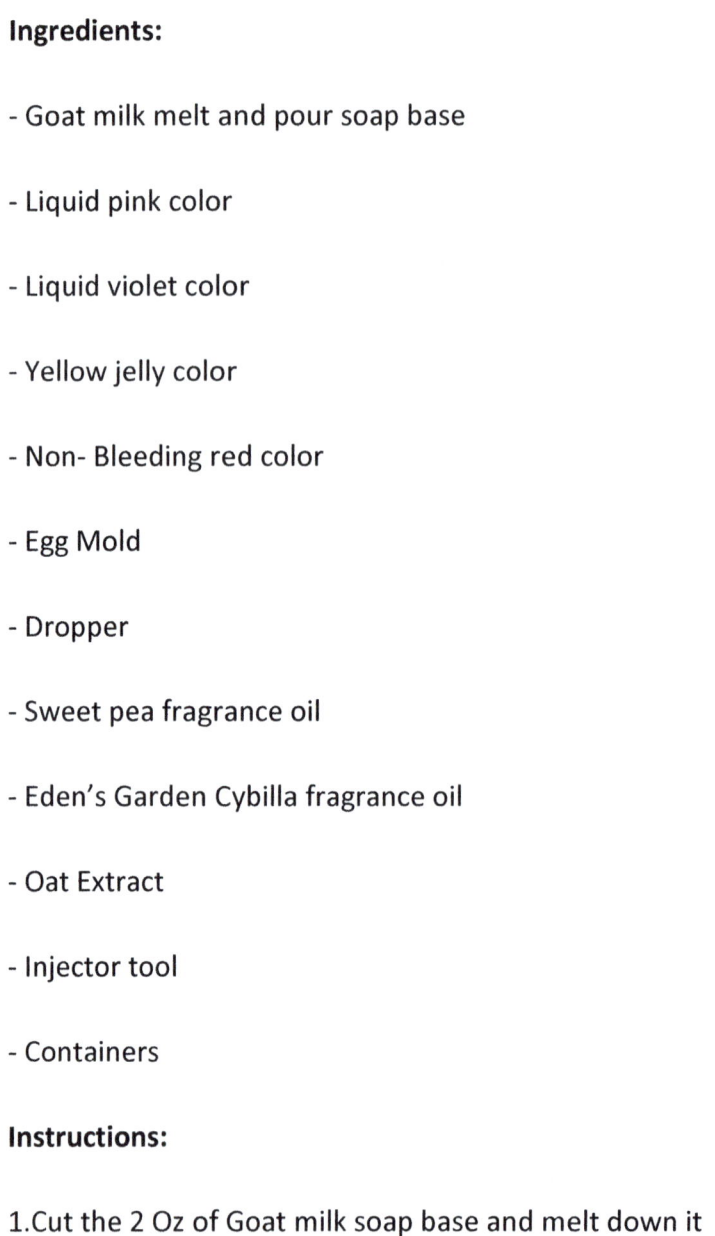

Ingredients:

- Goat milk melt and pour soap base

- Liquid pink color

- Liquid violet color

- Yellow jelly color

- Non- Bleeding red color

- Egg Mold

- Dropper

- Sweet pea fragrance oil

- Eden's Garden Cybilla fragrance oil

- Oat Extract

- Injector tool

- Containers

Instructions:

1.Cut the 2 Oz of Goat milk soap base and melt down it into microwave with 6 seconds burst. Now take the

Egg mold and using injector tool pour the white base in a mold first divot. Spray with isopropyl alcohol to disperse the bubble and allow it to settle down for 10 – 15 minutes.

2. Keep a cup of hot water nearby to clean the injector tool after every use to prevent blockage of injector. As soap gets hardened the injector get blocked, so rinse thoroughly with warm water to prevent clogging on soap into the injector.

3. Now cut the 6 Oz of goat milk soap base and melt it into microwave with 6 seconds burst. Now pour the melted base into three containers so that each container contains 2 Oz of soap base.

4. Now add three colors into these three containers like that:

4 -6 drops of liquid violet in one container

5 -7 drops of liquid pink with 1 drop of non-bleeding red in one container

4 – 6 drops of jelly yellow in another container.

5. Stir thoroughly to mix the colors completely with the melted soap base.

6. Now take the three mold in which you have previously dropped the white base. On white base drops add each color melted soap base drops using injector tool. Now spray with alcohol to disperse bubble and keep the mold aside to settle down for 10 – 15 minutes.

7. Once the soap base in cooled down in the molds, Now it's time to pour different color melted soap over different colors. But before that you have to melt the three containers again in microwave with 5 seconds burst, as it may have hardened again.

8. After the all three mixture get melted in microwave now , again take the three molds in which you have already filled the first divot with drops of white and colored soap base.

9. Now pour the little bit melted soap of pink color into the container having yellow drops in it. Pour the violet color melted soap from the container into the mold containing pink color drops and pour the yellow color melted soap base into the mold containing pink color drops. You can choose the combination and colors of your choice, the colors used by us is according to our

own choice but you can easily customize it according to your requirements and wish.

10. Now keep aside the three mold to cool down again for 10 – 15 minutes.

11. Simultaneously, cut 9 Oz of goat milk soap base and melt it down in the microwave for 10 seconds bursts. Do not add any color in it. Add in it 3 ml oat Extract, 1ml of sweet pea fragrance and 2ml of Eden's Garden Fragrance. Stir the mixture thoroughly to mix the contents well.

12. Now, if the soap in the mold has cooled down, pour this colorless and fragrance rich mixture into three molds with equal proportion of 2 – 3 Oz in each. Spray with isopropyl Alcohol to disperse bubbles and keep the molds aside to settle down and cool.

13. Now take the colored goat milk soap base containers, add in each container 1 Oz of more melted goat milk soap base with few drops of colors and 5 ml of sweet pea fragrance oil, 1ml of Oat Extract and 5ml of Eden's Garden fragrance oil. Then mix all the contents together.

14. Now take the mold with cool down white base and add in each mold the color mixture which you have previously poured in it. Add the violet color goat milk soap mixture in violet mold, in pink color adds the pink color and in yellow add the yellow.

15. Spray with isopropyl alcohol and keep the mold to cool down for at 130 degree or below for 30 – 60 minutes.

16. Once cooled unmold the soap and use it as you want.

17. This is an embellish soap recipe with beautiful colors and eggs look. You can keep it in the bathrooms of your kids to attract them dwelling a healthy habit of washing hands and even you can use them as Easter gifts to your family and friends.

18. This easy and quick soap recipe will help you attain the great appreciation not only at your home but in your social circle too. So, your Easter soap with beautiful fragrances.

4. Anti-bacterial Melt and Pour Soap Recipe

This is an easy to make and use anti-bacterial soap, quite good for kids and people doing a lot chores require deep cleaning and protection from germs. Like working in forms, gardens, at home and working persons and school going kids. You will find it quite handy to make and satisfying to use. So here we go with the quick and instant anti-bacterial soap.

Ingredients:

-Melt and pour soap base (Both clear and opaque)

-Green coloring (you can use any color of your choice)

-Goat milk powder

-Dessert essence tree oil

-Eucalyptus essential oil

-Polysorbate 20

-Stearic acid

-Dried eucalyptus leaves

Directions to prepare:

1.Take a handful of eucalyptus leaves and put into spice grinder, ground it till become a fine powder.

2. Melt down the clear melt and pour soap base, add in it green coloring and eucalyptus and stir it till mixed together well.

3. Take the opaque melt and pour soap base and melt it down. Add in it the stearic acid, polysorbate 20, eucalyptus essential oil, tea tree essential oil , and goat milk powder. Stir the mixture well until combined together.

4. Now take a mold of your choice, pour into both the clear and opaque melt and pour soap bases, whether in layers and in half proportion.

5. Keep the mold to cool down in low temperature.

6. Unmold the soap and cut it into bars if required and use it to protect yourself and your family from germs.

This could be a great addition in germ protection kit especially in summers. So, try it out at home and see how it turn out to be your greatest germ protection soap.

5. Swirl Melt and Pour Cubes Soap Recipe

You can easily give your homemade soaps a professionally manufactured look by trying out this wonderful soap recipe. This swirl soap is not attract you to use it again and again, but its charming fragrance will provide a refreshing sensation and keep you active for long after taking bath from this easily made soap.

Ingredients:

- 16 Oz of white soap base

- 32 Oz of clear soap base

- tangerine wow pigment (1 teaspoon)

- 1 Oz of cherry blossom fragrance oil

- electric bubble gum pigment (1 teaspoon)

- 3 Tbsp. liquid glycerin

- fired up fuchsia pigment (1 teaspoon)

- Silicon cubes mold

Tools Required:

- 3 containers (heat safe)

- Spray bottle

- Mini mixer

- Mini scoops

Directions:

1. First prepare the coloring for the soaps, for it take 1 tbsp. of melted glycerin for each color like:

-1 tbsp. of melted glycerin base and add in it 1 teaspoon of electric bubblegum.

-1 tbsp. of melted glycerin base and add in it 1 teaspoon of Tangerine wow.

-1 tbsp. of melted glycerin base and add in it 1 teaspoon of fired Up Fuchsia.

2. Now mix the colors well with the glycerin mixture and set aside for later use. For better mixing blend the colors with the glycerin mixture using a mini mixer. Make sure to mix the color a bit before turning on the mini mixer to avoid pink cloud of colorant and to prevent airing out of the color.

3. Take the 32 Oz. of clear soap base and melt it down in the microwave with 30 seconds of bursts until fully liquid. Add in it .25 Oz of cherry blossom fragrance oil.

4. Now separate this clear soap liquid into two containers. Take the previously prepared colorants. Add the 10 drops of glycerin and tangerine colorant in the first container containing melted soap base. Stir the mixture well and cover with plastic cover to keep it warm.

5. Take the other container containing melted soap base, add in it the 8 drops of bubblegum and glycerin colorant mixture. Stir it well, cover it with plastic and keep aside.

6. Now take the 16 Oz of white base soap. Melt it into the microwave oven on a 30 second burst until liquefy completely. Add in it 8 drops of fired up fuchsia and .75 Oz of cherry blossom fragrance oil and also glycerin pigment. Stir the mixture well until combined.

7. Let all the three container to cool down till the temperature 130 – 135 degrees. You keep them covered until cool or even use a spoon to cool them

down until they reached the temperature of 130 degrees.

8. Now it's time to show the soap mixing magic. Take the cubes mold. Pour into it some amount of orange soap mixture. Now take pink soap mixture and add a little pink mixture on the top of the orange mixture layer.

Tip: Pour the mixture into the opposite corners of the cubes to give different color variations.

9. Now take the container containing the opaque pink soap and pour it into cubes over pink soap mixture. Also try to pour it into opposite corners of the cubes to bring more variation in the color and designs.

10. Keep pouring the mixture until all cubes get filled or mixture get finished.

11. Pouring in corners will create a swirl effect, do not just pour one layer over others as it will create more layering effect than swirls. As we are not looking for acquiring layering effect, so just spray alcohol to disperse any bubble created while pouring mixture.

12. You have to be quick in pouring the one mixture over the other to avoid layers to settle down. This swirl magic effect can only be attained at temperature 130 – 13 degree, so be careful about the temperature of the mixtures while pouring them into the mold.

13.Keep the mold to cool down for 5 -6 hours. Once the soap is cooled down unmold the soap and use it as your requirement. You can also use this amazing soap cubes as Christmas gifts for your family and friends.

6. Tea Rose Beauty Soap Recipe

It is an anti-bacterial facial soap, which not only good to provide moisturizing protection to your skin, but also keep you healthy and germ free.

Ingredients:

- 5 drops tea tree oil

- 10 drops rose E.O

- 4 Oz melt and pour soap base

- Red color

- ½ tablespoon Jojoba Oil

Directions:

Take the 4 Oz melt and pour soap base and melt in until completely liquid. Now add in it the 5 drops of tea tree oil and 10 drops of rose E.O. Mix the mixture slowly so bubbles will not form. Now add red color and jojoba oil in the mixture and stir it until combined well. Now pour this mixture into the mold of your choice, whether its round or rectangle or of any shape. Let the mixture settle down and cool. Unmold the mixture, your anti-bacterial beauty soap is ready to use!

7. Mint Leaf Soap Recipe

A great soap to keep your refresh and cool in this hot summer weather.

Ingredients:

- White Melt and pour soap base

- Mint leaves

- Sparkling accent glitter

- Green color

- Mint fragrance oil

- 3 Oz of transparent melt and pour soap base

Directions:

First Step:

First take the white melt and pour soap base, cut and melt it till liquid. Add the 1 – 2 drops of green color and mix it well. Add in it mint fragrance oil and sparkling accent glitter. Mix the mixture well. Pour this mixture into mint leaf mold. Keep it in refrigerator to cool down for 10 – 15 minutes. Once cooled, unmold it to use it within other soap just going to prepare.

Second Step:

Now take the transparent soap base and melt it down until complete liquid. Now add in it the green color to give a light greenish look and mint fragrance oil. Stir it well. Now take the mold, place in it the leaf mint soap prepared already in first step, and pour over it this mixture of transparent soap base. Now keep the mold to cool down for 10 – 15 minutes. Once it settles down and cooled, unmold the soap and use it in hot summer to give you the cool effect and keep you safe from harshness of weather. Enjoy this pretty easy recipe of mint soap with beautiful mint leaf design.

8. Beautiful Color Layered Soap Recipe

Ingredients:

- 15 Oz of white melt and pour soap base

- 40 Oz of clear base of pour and melt soap

- Super pearly white mica

- 1.1 OZ of plumeria fragrance oil

- Diluted Tropical orange lab color

- Diluted Pink Lab Color

Directions:

1. Take both the white and clear melt and pour soap base, cut them down into 1 inch chunks and keep them both into separate containers.

2. Now melt the clear soap base in microwave for 30 seconds bursts until the soap base gets melted completely. Add in it 2 mini scoops of super pearly mica. Mix the solution well. The super pearly mica will give the clear soap a shimmer effect and enhance the coloration charm. Use the isopropyl alcohol to disperse any bubble formed over the soap surface.

3. Add the 0.8 Oz of Plumeria Fragrance into the solution and stir well. Now divide the solution into two equal parts. In one part add 5 ml diluted tropical orange color and mix well. To the other part also add 3ml of diluted pink color and mix the solution well.

4. For keeping the proportion of layers equal and balance. Further divide the each solution into 10 Ounces. This way you won't have to worry about the layers thickness and all goes well and balanced.

5. Take the mold and pour into the pink color solution to form the first layer. Spray the isopropyl alcohol on the surface to disperse the bubbles. Now, settle down the solution to get hardened.

6. Now check the temperature of orange solution, if it's below 125 degrees, then pour this layer over first pink color layer in the mold. Make sure to spray the alcohol over pink layer before pouring orange solution to ensure the both layers get stick together firmly. Temperature of orange solution is important, if it is too hot then it will melt down the pink layer too and will cause some undesirable effects. To avoid it, better check the temperature before pouring out the orange layer over pink.

7. Take the white melt and pour soap base and heat it in microwave with 30 seconds bursts. Make sure it completely melts down. Now add in it 2 mini scoops of super pearly mica to add shimmer effect in the solution. Also add in it the 0.3 Oz of Plumeria fragrance oil. Mix the solution well until all the content combined together.

8. Once the white soap reached the desirable cool temperature, spray alcohol over orange layer in the mold and pour over it this white soap solution. Keep it aside to cool down. Once it gets cool, you can pour more layers over it first pour orange solution and then the pink solution over it. This will give the soap a layering effect which we want. You can use any color or your choice to make it more desirable to you and your family.

9. Make sure to always spray alcohol before pouring any layer over the previous to ensure a firm bond of one layer with another. Allow the layers to settle and cool down. Unmold the soap and enjoy your favorite color soap to beautify yourself and your family.

Some Quick Tips to Layering Melt and pour soap

Mostly, people get troubled, when it comes to make layered soaps at home. Although, the layered soaps seems more desirable and at the same time difficult to handle. Following these quick tips will save your effort and time:

1. Before pouring the second layer over the first one, make sure the first layer is hardened enough to support the weight of the second layer.

2. Always spray the alcohol over first layer to ensure adherence of first layer with the second. It will also help to get rid of the dust particles which cause problems while layering the soap.

3. be careful about the temperature of second solution you are pouring over first one. If it is too hot it will melt down the first layer too, and can disrupt the proper layering effect.

4. Making soap in cool environment will also cause a lot of trouble, as it becomes hard for first layer to stick to the other in cold temperature and if you are facing problem of cracking then it's better to prepare your layering soap in a warm environment to avoid any inconvenience.

9. Oat Meal Recipe

Ingredients:

- 8 Oz of Clear Melt and pour soap base

- ½ Oz of Oatmeal

- 8 Oz of white melt and pour soap base

- 2 Scoops of honey beige mica

- ½ Oz of oatmeal, honey and milk fragrance

Directions:

1. Take 8 Oz of white and 8 Oz of clear melt and pour soap bases, melt down both with the 30 seconds burst in microwave until completely turned into liquid. Then add in it 2 mini scoops of honey beige mica.

2. Take ½ Oz of oatmeal and grind it into a grinder for 5 seconds until get smooth and fine. It will also give an exfoliator touch to soap. Grind it till the particles get smaller and easier to settle down in soap without creating any rough look.

3. Now add in it ½ Oz of milk, honey and Oatmeal fragrance oil. Mix in it well to combine them properly.

4. Add the oatmeal in the solution and stir well. Then wait for 2 minutes until oatmeal does not get settle down in the base. If it is, then your base is not enough hard to evenly distribute the oatmeal. Stir and wait for base to get little bit thick to support oatmeal suspension.

5. Now take the mold and pour the solution into it. Set aside to cool down. Unmold the soap and enjoy the soap with exfoliation to get the smoother and shiny skin each day.

 These instant and customizable melt and pour soap recipes are best to try at home as the creative hobby and even you can involve your kids in soap making process, to make their summer worth spending. These soaps will not only provide you the freedom to choose your desirable fragrance and color, but also the ingredients which are best suitable according to your skin type. You can use these soaps for yourself and even can gift others.

Thank You Page

I want to personally thank you for reading my book. I hope you found information in this book useful and I would be very grateful if you could leave your honest review about this book. I certainly want to thank you in advance for doing this.